Self-Esteem

Hypnosis For Enhancing Self-Esteem And Boosting Confidence

(Conquer Feelings Of Insecurity, Enhance Confidence, And Embrace Your Authentic Self)

Lewis Patterson

TABLE OF CONTENT

What Is Self-Esteem 1

Embark On The Path Of Self-Discovery Commencing Now 8

Leadership And Extroversion 35

Approaching Motivation 59

Perpetual Self-Enhancement Is The Key To Success 88

Embark On Your Quest For Self-Discovery Starting Today 111

When Is It Appropriate To Exhibit Extroverted Behaviors? 134

What Is Self-Esteem

Self-esteem refers to an individual's perception and evaluation of oneself. If you have consistently received notions that you possess a lack of dexterity and internalized these notions, you will perceive yourself as being inept. The reality is that much of the feedback we receive throughout our lives is not malicious in nature, but rather has the potential to have a lasting impact on us for a significant period of time. For instance, my mother consistently failed to recognize any of my endeavors as meaningful or valuable. During my formative years, my conviction was shaped by the perception that I possessed a deficiency in comparison to my peers, as none of my efforts received acknowledgement. Acknowledgment is not a requisite for our confidence, although it does contribute positively. When consistently neglected for our positive contributions, we have a tendency to incline towards a negative perspective. We experience a sense of dissatisfaction with our identity and, when confronted with novel challenges, frequently encounter setbacks as a result of our inherent self-doubt.

This phenomenon may manifest from an early age, even during one's toddler years, and although it is unlikely that one's parents would purposefully inflict such circumstances, it unfortunately occurs. An analogous phenomenon occurs within educational institutions. You are subject to comparisons with your peers and you may perceive that you fall short of your own personal standards. You do not possess the same level of physical attractiveness as others. You do not possess a talent for athletic activities. You lack the capability to engage in activities undertaken by others. The issue lies in the perpetual existence of individuals who excel in certain aspects of their lives, surpassing one's own achievements. You cannot evade the matter, therefore, how do you confront it? Indeed, it hinges on the extent to which that unfavorable perception of you is reinforced.

Consequently, when individuals repeatedly assert a particular notion, it ingrains itself as truth within your belief system, subsequently influencing your mindset in alignment with that narrative. Have you ever encountered individuals who became ensnared in a destructive, abusive relationship? When you lack confidence and self-esteem, you think you are entitled to less than others and so settle for less. Vulnerable individuals tend to possess a strong allure for individuals inclined towards abusive behavior, and regrettably, even when these individuals extricate themselves from such relationships, if their sense of self-worth remains unfavorable, it is likely that subsequent relationships will yield similar detrimental effects. This occurrence is primarily rooted in the fact that individuals tend to reinforce and perpetuate their own self-perception over the course of their lifetime. If one believes that their value is no greater than the challenges presented to them by life, they may find contentment in accepting small portions of success due to a belief that it is all they are deserving of. I have an update to share with you. While this may have been customary for you, it does not render it mandatory. One has the ability to alter their own perception of their identity and concurrently develop self-esteem and confidence.

Firstly, let us examine the deleterious consequences stemming from challenges in self-esteem:

- You do not place a high value on your self-worth.
- One refrains from indulging in items or experiences that one believes are not warranted.
- You hold the belief that you are entitled to a lesser share in life compared to others.
- You compromise on subpar relationships • You accept inadequate

relationships • You make do with unsatisfactory relationships • You tolerate mediocre relationships
• You compromise on positions that fail to showcase your full potential.

At a certain juncture in one's life, it becomes necessary to emancipate oneself from the shackles of negativity. Upon doing so, one has the opportunity to cultivate confidence, as confidence tends to operate in such a manner. When an individual successfully accomplishes a task with excellence, they experience a sense of personal satisfaction and elevated self-esteem. If one remains convinced of their own inability to accomplish more, they will solely experience a realm filled with dull and average undertakings. In a measure, this internal depiction of your identity is determining the manner in which you conduct your life.

Consequently, it can be inferred that self-esteem exerts significant influence over the overall quality of an individual's life. When the standard is set at a low level, limited anticipation is present, resulting in minimal outcomes. If one possesses a high level of self-regard, they demonstrate a significant degree of self-assuredness and determination in their endeavors, enabling them to pursue their goals with utmost confidence. There is another prong in the fork as well. Individuals who exhibit excessive self-assurance tend to approach tasks with a careless and hasty attitude, inevitably resulting in errors. This behavior can be attributed to their inflated perception of their own competence, which often shields them from the impact of constructive criticism on their self-esteem. Critique in and of itself does not entail any harm. It facilitates personal growth, fosters the establishment of individual boundaries, and promotes learning. However, exclusively employing it for self-judgment unduly undermines self-esteem and confidence.

Throughout the upcoming chapters, we will delve into the occurrences, causes, and strategies to address the adverse implications of diminished self-esteem and lack of confidence. This comprehensive exploration aims to equip you with a heightened awareness of the detrimental effects on your personal growth, with the ultimate goal of fostering enduring self-improvement. The perspective in which you perceive your own life plays a significant role, just as the manner in which individuals criticize and belittle you does. Once one attains self-mastery, the validation of others becomes unnecessary, thus allowing for the cultivation and thriving of self-esteem. Rest assured, you have the ability to manage this situation. However, it is imperative that you acquire the necessary knowledge on how to do so.

Embark On The Path Of Self-Discovery Commencing Now

Your pursuit of self-improvement will prove to be challenging. It will present a multitude of obstacles, forcing you to encounter numerous circumstances that may continually cause you to reevaluate your own value. Do not hesitate, as ultimately, you will gain a more profound understanding and appreciation of your own capabilities.

Self-esteem and self-confidence develop gradually, requiring dedicated and sustained efforts. It will test your patience and expose you to numerous instances of trial and error. It is imperative to recognize that the concept of flawless self-esteem is non-existent. Individuals who possess unwavering confidence are aware of the possibility and inevitability of failure. Please acknowledge and embrace this aspect of your being; furthermore, it is advisable to fully embrace your entire self, understanding that you possess both strengths and weaknesses, just like any other human being. The key is to change your perspective from considering yourself as lacking value to recognizing your vast untapped capabilities.

It constitutes a lengthy expedition, a demanding one. There may arise occasions when you encounter setbacks and disappointments, yet it is through these challenges that you will acquire the necessary fortitude to endure and grow. As you are currently engaged in a deliberate endeavor to elevate yourself, you will cultivate a heightened mindfulness of your personal experiences. With the acquired expertise found within the contents of this literary work, you shall possess the necessary resources to confront personal challenges, the sustenance to persevere, and the drive to sustain your quest towards self-improvement.

Amidst the adversities encountered, it is imperative to consistently acknowledge and seize upon even the smallest fragments of uplifting encounters. Please make a record of your minor achievements and use them as a foundation for further progress. Employ them as a catalyst for personal improvement. These small yet remarkable elements embody true brilliance, and it is essential to treasure and value them sincerely. These are the fruits of your own diligent efforts and unwavering determination. In times of adversity and desolation, reflect upon the favorable occurrences of your voyage and allow those luminary instances to provide illumination and guidance.

We earnestly aspire that this book has bestowed upon you profound perspectives on cultivating your self-esteem and confidence as an individual, transcending mere gender distinctions. The entire globe eagerly anticipates your arrival, fully aware of the invaluable blessings you bring forth. Over time, you will reflect upon this expedition of introspection and personal growth with a smile gracing your countenance and an assured tranquility to proclaim "I have accomplished it!"

Chapter 6: The Primary Method for Cultivating Self-Confidence

Prior to fully engaging, allow me to clarify one important point. Subsequently, the forthcoming details will assist you in constructing an individualized framework aimed at enhancing your self-assurance. I cannot overemphasize the significance of the notion of 'personal framework'. This specific framework serves as a support system or framework to facilitate the development of your self-confidence. Put simply, it is necessary for you to complete this framework by providing specific details derived from your personal experiences. Only you know that.

Through providing you with these comprehensive principles, you can subsequently incorporate the specifics by considering your unique circumstances, personal background, and individual inclinations. You must avoid relying on universally applicable or miraculous confidence-building 'remedies'. The majority of these alternatives cannot be regarded as viable solutions, as what may prove effective for one individual may not yield the same outcome for another. Consequently, it is notably more advantageous to collaborate within the confines of a structured framework. Sufficient details within the frame prompt the recollection of specific events unfolding in one's life. You can subsequently incorporate personal information and subsequently adjust them as you implement the framework.

The key to the framework lies in its consistent implementation. Through consistent practice, you can subsequently identify the aspects that are effective and subsequently make adjustments to those that are not. Through diligent implementation and a significant investment of time, one can achieve the refinement of a framework tailored to suit their unique lifestyle. It is neither mine nor another individual's, but rather your own life. This serves as the pivotal determinant of accomplishing success.

Once more, exercise caution when it comes to relying on purportedly 'magical' checklists for developing confidence. They frequently encounter failure due to their reliance on the experiences of others. Those individuals possess distinct experiences from your own. Those individuals could be encountering diverse situations compared to yours. How can their proposed solution, when analyzed in a detailed and systematic manner and implemented in a business setting, be beneficial for your organization? It is simply not feasible. It is attempting to forcibly reconcile incompatible elements.

Conversely, employ the prescribed structure and adapt it according to your unique circumstances. I would like to clarify this matter as it is crucial to avoid the temptation of seeking shortcuts or 'magical' solutions that promise exceptional outcomes simply by following a set of steps or tips. They rarely do. It is imperative that you dedicate yourself and exert effort in that endeavor. You have to customise. It is imperative to tailor the solutions in order to effectively address the unique circumstances that pertain to you. Alternatively, if you choose otherwise, you would be accepting a significantly diminished amount, representing only a fraction of the original value, at best, and experiencing a complete failure, at worst. With that being stated, let us commence.

The predominant method for cultivating self-assurance entails engaging in social situations with an air of confidence. This is the common advice suggested by numerous other literary sources. It is advisable to proceed directly and project an air of confidence in that particular situation. Simply observe individuals who exude confidence, diligently analyze their non-verbal cues, and subsequently emulate those very signals. What this all boils down to is fake it until you make it. You are aware of its falsehood because, at a profound level, you experience a sense of inadequacy. Internally, you harbor a sense of inherent insignificance, yet outwardly, you portray an air of unwavering self-assurance and superiority. You demonstrate a proactive demeanor and possess a profound and unwavering belief in your abilities.

The merits of the 'fake it until you make it' approach are readily apparent. It is quick. It can be feasibly executed. In your professional setting, it is highly likely that there exists a minimum of one individual who possesses a notable level of confidence. One simply needs to observe an individual from a distance, carefully analyze their behavior, language, body movements, and even their overall appearance, and then proceed to replicate those attributes. Adopting a confident demeanor without the necessary groundwork often requires minimal prior arrangement. You have the ability to make spontaneous decisions. One may derive inspiration from recalling a memory of encountering a self-assured individual during their time in education or at a prior place of employment. Subsequently, you direct the focus of your social interactions towards that individual in the present moment. It pertains to an unrestrictive approach in expressing assurance.

An notable drawback of feigning competence until achieving proficiency is that it necessitates a process of experimentation and correction. As previously stated, what proves successful for one individual may not yield the same results for yourself. They might be exhibiting distinct indications and executing it impeccably. They possess an unparalleled expertise in exuding such self-assurance; notwithstanding, were you to attempt the same, you could potentially experience a humiliating setback. It is possible that you could elevate the level of foolishness exhibited by your actions.

Regrettably, engaging in a process of trial and error without due caution can lead to committing errors that may lead to an extended period of time required for emotional recovery. It is exceedingly common to experience trauma when attempting to deceive, as one is merely simulating competence until genuine proficiency is achieved. In the end, it is conceivable that you may experience a severe failure that could potentially lead you to adopt maladaptive strategies for coping with criticism. One can develop a tendency towards shyness; one may adopt a highly judgmental mindset. One can establish a mindset whereby 'taking a proactive approach is the most effective means of protection.' Put differently, your attempt to conceal your dearth of self-assurance is manifested through the adoption of an offensive or arrogant demeanor. I strongly believe that it was apparent to you how these coping mechanisms exacerbate issues rather than effectively addressing them.

Chapter 6

Overcoming Negative Thinking

Each individual possesses an inherent capacity for creativity, which may occasionally remain concealed and fail to manifest itself prominently.

Additionally, by delving into professional practices, one can effectively foster ingenuity at a comparable speed as compared to others.

Discovered and currently engaged in exploring your potential for innovation, with the aim of showcasing it at the forefront of our operations. Here

Below are a few key suggestions to assist you in stimulating your creativity and nurturing your ability to think innovatively.

ness.

• Generate documentation – you can actively explore your creativity and engage that aspect of your mind

By creating a comprehensive list whenever you encounter an issue that necessitates innovative solutions.

In order to engage in conservative speculation, please compile a comprehensive list encompassing an equivalent number of ideas pertaining to arrangements.

Allow your creativity to flow freely.

- Continuously adapt and evolve throughout your lifetime – occasionally, we may encounter creative obstacles in our path.

In the circumstance where we find ourselves entangled in an inescapable pattern, make alterations to your current situation.

Gradually, we strive to reestablish the flow of channels in our daily existence.

- Address the inadequately thought-out ideas, regardless of whether you are only contemplating their implementation.

In terms of practical ideas, it appears that you are still in the realm of imagination. Therefore, it would be advisable to focus on the unfavorable concepts and work on refining them.

Establishing them, the assertion that it is an imprudent notion, regardless, may potentially evolve into...

A remarkable solution and response to your concerns.

- Engage in a remarkable collaborative environment where team members brainstorm collectively and generate insightful ideas together.

An exceptional approach for fostering ingenuity.

• Push yourself and others to strive for improvement – if you challenge

Reveal to oneself that one is unable to achieve something in the manner in which it is intended.

Once you have successfully accomplished it, you will then need to contemplate alternative approaches.

Devise innovative solutions to circumvent the problem.

• Scribble - in the event that you find yourself lacking ideas for a solution, then

Ensure you have a pen and paper readily available and allow your imaginative mind to freely express itself by sketching out your thoughts.

It is truly remarkable the thoughts that will emerge when one liberates their mind.

these lines.

• Stimulate the cognitive hemisphere of your cerebrum – the right hemisphere of your brain is the

Nurture and invigorate the power of imagination through the act of enacting and harnessing its potential.

Attempt taking a few breaths exclusively through your left nostril, focusing on the left side.

- Engage the services of a comprehensive mentor - should you perceive a true deficiency in your creative ability

If you find yourself depleted at that juncture, it may be prudent to contemplate engaging the services of a holistic mentor to aid in guiding your thoughts.

In this regard, a comprehensive mentor can aid you in identifying the areas where you may need improvement

Imagination is lacking and I am willing to collaborate with you to strengthen it.

responsibilities and adopt a carefree and youthful mindset.

Children possess superior cognitive abilities and possess limitless creative imaginations that enable them to overcome stress and reconnect with the essence of their youth.

no limits, take on a similar mindset as a kid at the point when you are stuck for inventive

Emotions and ideas will soon flow unrestricted once again.

stress or pressure.

Under significant duress, acquiring knowledge of a decompression method offers a sense of relief.

Can provide mental clarity, afford a fresh start, and stimulate your creative faculties.

once more.

- Employ psychological tactics - keep a few strategic mind games at your disposal, such as logical reasoning

Solving puzzles diverts your mind from worries, fostering an analytical mindset whereby pondering and reflecting upon a riddle fosters constructive and innovative thinking.

Creativity tips and resources

Each individual stands to benefit from incorporating creativity into their daily lives. You may employ ingenuity to assist in tasks.

business endeavors, goal establishment, household and family management, and numerous additional aspects. To help with the

To enhance your creativity in the majority of your domestic and professional endeavors, presented below are 10 recommendations.

1. Stay Healthy

Uncover a preferred activity schedule and adhere to it diligently. Alter it as and when necessary.

notwithstanding, persist in engaging in a specific form of activity. Rest soundly. Consume a variety of nutritious sustenance.

ments. Meditation or engaging in activities that bring you enjoyment and promote relaxation can aid in maintaining your mental well-being.

mind centered.

2. Explore New Things

We effectively accomplish numerous tasks without deliberately contemplating their execution. These things become our

Routine daily agendas - the mundane and tiresome. Attempt to undertake a novel endeavor. It is highly plausible that this could involve something as trivial as opting for an alternative commuting route.

Enrolling in a course that pertains to a subject you have harbored a strong desire to acquire knowledge in for quite a significant period.

3. Adopting an Inquisitive Mindset, Similar to That of Curious George

Pose interrogative reflections pertaining to all visual, auditory, and literary stimuli encountered. Why? How? What if? Discover the

Resolution to your queries. You may also consider maintaining a journal of inquiry and meticulously recording all

your discoveries.

4. Read a New Book

Select an option that deviates from your typical choice. Acquire a copy from the library. In the circumstance that you possess

Should one consistently strive for a deeper comprehension of reality, it is advisable to gravitate towards works of nonfiction. There is an abundant quantity

There is a diverse selection of captivating literature available for exploration, encompassing a wide array of genres to select from. Your custodian will be pleased

to aid you in the exploration of unfamiliar literary works.

5. Act Like a Kid

Children possess a delightful and carefree nature that is both genuine and enjoyable. Take into account the achievements you made without a specific purpose.

rationale during a person's youth Create a visual representation, retrieve the charcoal materials, gather some finger paints, proceed to

Attend the local gathering of events and activities suitable for children. Enjoy the plethora of offerings and have a delightful time.

time!

6. Everyone Requires Some Period of Solitude

Allocate a portion of your regular schedule for the sole purpose of unwinding. You may employ reflection should you desire.

to think. Please refrain from making any arrangements or settling any financial obligations, whatsoever. Simply fail to help

a short time. 7. What If?

What if tomorrow marked the culmination of mankind? "Consider a hypothetical situation where you attended a educational institution for

business. Take into account the potential that individuals from outside may have been sincere. "Take into account the potential that there

is a hereafter. Use your imagination to envision a situation in which you formulate inquiries and solely witness the proceedings.

Wherever your thoughts may wander.

8. Never Assume Anything

Anticipating outcomes typically places individuals in challenging circumstances. It is to be anticipated that your

Being a manager is relatively easy. Envision a situation wherein he displays complete apathy towards his own existence and hastily brings it to an end.

imposing demands on his employees." or "placing excessive burdens on his staff. You can anticipate that the individual who merged in front of you earlier today

was discourteous. Envision a situation wherein they were expeditiously escorting their juvenile to the emergency room.

gency clinic.

9. Write About You

Who are you? How would you describe your personal attributes? May I inquire about the location where you have held a significant position?

An integral component of your existence? When do the most impactful events occur within the course of your life? For what reason

Do you achieve objectives in the manner in which you currently employ? Can you elaborate on how you intend to proceed with

Do you engage in the activities of your daily life on a regular basis?

10. Have Conversations with People

Hear attentively to their expressions rather than awaiting your opportunity to speak. What characteristics must this individual possess? Visualize their lifestyle and thought processes.

Leadership And Extroversion

Numerous notable and successful figures serve as evidence that individuals possessing introverted tendencies possess the capability to excel as leaders. In addition to the aforementioned individuals listed within the pages of this book, other notable figures who exhibit introverted tendencies include Abraham Lincoln, Eleanor Roosevelt, Charles Darwin, and Steven Spielberg. Individuals who demonstrate boldness and vigor are often inclined to attain a prominent position and showcase self-assurance in articulating their ideas. However, it should be acknowledged that such attributes do not necessarily guarantee the possession of effective leadership qualities.

In accordance with the organizational framework, there exist certain companies and types of industries where introverted individuals may not be optimally suited. However, the way how most people view extroverts as superior to their more silent counterpart is wrong. The attributes exhibited by both individuals are fundamental in constituting a harmonious organization. Rather than engaging in a dispute over who possesses superior leadership skills, it would be more beneficial for both factions to seek common ground and collaborate harmoniously. However, despite this, the social stigma surrounding introverts continues to exist, underscoring the importance of acknowledging the common characteristics they share with effective leadership.

Many individuals hold the belief that introverts lack the necessary vocal abilities of extroverts, thus questioning their capacity to effectively lead, inspire, and steer their teams. One admirable aspect of these reticent individuals is their cleverness in departing from conventions and attaining comparable, or occasionally superior, outcomes.

Qualities of Introversion that Contribute to Effective Leadership

1. Good Listeners.

Extroverts exhibit a unidirectional thought process, as previously elucidated, as they adhere to a consensually accepted predetermined framework of guidelines and protocols. Their responses and choices are predicated upon this, resulting in their propensity to resist embracing novel concepts on a frequent basis. Conversely, introverted individuals actively listen to suggestions and meticulously contemplate these concepts.

However, compatibility continues to be of paramount importance in ensuring the effectiveness and efficiency of a collective endeavor. According to a study conducted by Francesca Gino, an associate professor at Harvard School of Business, teams headed by introverted leaders and consisting of proactive subordinates possess the potential for remarkable success. Similarly, employers who dominate conversations are more suitably paired with passive subordinates who prefer receiving explicit instructions.

2. Ability to Focus.

The contemporary society we inhabit is greatly inundated with various distractions, making it decidedly arduous to maintain focus and concentration on any given task. As introverts possess an inherent affinity for solitariness, they exhibit no apprehension when confronted with the prospect of being alone with their thoughts. Engaging in cognitive processes enhances their mental acuity and refines their aptitude for concentration.

During business meetings, introverted superiors may maintain a reserved demeanor, appearing disinterested and detached. However, beneath their outward calmness, they are actively assimilating and analyzing all the information and discussions taking place. An impressive aspect about them is their ability not only to assimilate the conveyed information, but also to engage in theorizing, envisioning, and strategizing simultaneously.

Issues are occasionally deliberated upon within the confines of the workplace, thereby causing a significant majority to become frequently diverted by the conspicuous matters at hand. It is often the unassuming leaders among us who uncover solutions, as they possess the ability to concentrate on the matter at hand and examine it from various perspectives.

3. Humble.

Jane T. In 2006, a comprehensive study on Servant Leadership was carried out by Wadell from Regent University. The research she conducted unveiled remarkable findings. She ascertained that there is an overlap between certain revered attributes of Servant Leadership and the intrinsic characteristics of introverts, among which humility stands out as one.

The notable characteristic of this leadership style lies in its ability to enable and encourage the development of followers. Individuals possessing these administrative attributes demonstrate a lack of interest in pursuing personal recognition and are not motivated by ego-driven endeavors. They hold the belief that by enhancing the capacities of their subordinates, they attain the pinnacle of their organizational potential.

4. Mild Tempered.

As previously stated, individuals with extroverted tendencies often verbalize their thoughts. Hence, whatever emotions they experience in the present moment, they will duly convey. Occasionally, an issue arises in this context when individuals are confronted with stress-inducing circumstances, as such situations can significantly exacerbate their temperament. This can be attributed to the fact that their energy consumption is derived from their surroundings. It follows that if the atmosphere is laden with heat, they will take in and manifest it accordingly.

In contrast, their polar counterparts are frequently composed and calm. In the presence of an introverted leader, an office characterized by disorder and tumultuousness will experience the restoration of order and tranquility, as the leader imparts a sense of serenity through their personal energy. This attribute is frequently disregarded by a significant number of individuals and is occasionally regarded as a deficiency, however, it possesses the potential to be the most formidable advantage of an individual with introverted tendencies. You exhibit a commendable level of composure and are not easily swayed by the dramatic events occuring in your presence. Indeed, you possess the ability to potentially alter these occurrences through the manifestation of appropriate energy.

5. Creates Meaningful Connections.

During conferences, it will become apparent as to whom the extroverted individuals are. They are individuals who display excessive levels of energy, transitioning between seats as they engage in conversations with various individuals. Indeed, while extroverts may amass a larger quantity of calling cards, one must question the extent to which the individuals they interacted with shall distinctly recollect their encounters. Conversely, their equivalents frequently confine their interactions to a select few individuals, however, in doing so, they cultivate a more profound connection.

It is frequently observed that individuals aspiring to advance in their professional pursuits are required to cultivate substantial professional connections. The primary consideration in this endeavor is to establish connections with a wide range of pertinent individuals, however, the crucial aspect lies in the cultivation of the rapport between the individual and their professional network. You may be acquainted with Mr. CEO as a result of a brief conversation, however, it is important to note that this does not establish a friendship. In order to classify this accurately, you and Mr. CEO are simply acquaintances. And one would be wise to avoid being relegated to the realm of mere acquaintanceship, for in doing so, one's visage and appellation may scarcely register within his memory.

Overcoming Introverted Characteristics to Enhance Leadership Abilities

In any given strength is an equivalent weakness. Indeed, the disposition of being introverted can yield benefits both in professional and personal spheres. Nevertheless, there will perpetually exist inherent attributes intended to counterbalance your seemingly superhuman characteristics. Typically, though, individuals tend to prioritize and excessively engage with these aspects, overshadowing the positive ones.

Reiterating these qualities can assist you in managing them, and unlock the radiance of your introverted strengths.

1. Leave your comfort zone.

Introverts tend to gravitate towards independent work as it aligns with their optimal functioning. Their cognitive capacity is optimized and their imaginative abilities are amplified, hence solitude provides them solace. Nonetheless, effective leadership necessitates consistent engagement and communication with individuals under one's authority. Venturing beyond one's comfort zone can prove challenging and awkward, nonetheless, it is imperative in order to cultivate enhanced leadership skills. One cannot depend solely on their intellectual capacity. Success also takes teamwork.

3.2 Acquire the Skills to Manage Your Emotions

Developing a mindset focused on optimism holds significant value in cultivating self-assurance and attaining harmony with one's surroundings. Positive thinking is making the best of difficult situations, reframing difficult things, completing a grief process, and holding yourself up through it. It is many things. Each individual will possess a unique perspective regarding the concept of positive thinking. There exist profound and manifold rationales that necessitate your acquisition of the skill of positive thinking. The connection between our mental state and physical well-being is intricately intertwined. There is a reciprocal relationship between the body and the mind; the body has a profound impact on one's thoughts and emotions. When an individual acquires the ability to cultivate persistent pessimistic thoughts that lead to the detriment of oneself and those around them, their overall being is subject to a deleterious impact. The encounter will render various aspects of your well-being, including muscle tension and immune functionality, significantly compromised.

Are you familiar with the idiom, "one's dietary choices influence their overall well-being"? There exists an alternative rendition of that statement that I derive pleasure from, which states: "Your thoughts shape your identity." When you harbor pessimistic thoughts regarding your own being, you are engaging in a form of self-deprecation and facilitating the realization of negative outcomes. By consistently affirming to oneself that they possess qualities of idleness and insignificance, they inadvertently promote engagement in actions that align with these perceptions of worthlessness or laziness. You begin to perceive yourself as embodying the most unfavorable version of your being. This is a matter that must be staunchly confronted. Positive thinking has a significantly more positive impact on one's overall health. Positive thinking will improve hour mood and attention span and even your physical health.

If you are experiencing symptoms indicative of an emotional disorder that are causing disruptions in your daily functioning, it could be of value to undergo an evaluation for mental health by a physician or another qualified healthcare provider. Depression is a prevalent phenomenon within our society, often stemming from disturbances or dysfunctions in mood regulation. Depression is an assemblage of symptomatic manifestations. These manifestations encompass a dearth of drive, sleep disturbances, excessive somnolence, decreased appetite or overeating, social withdrawal, and potential additional indicators. A significant factor is the absence of drive or motivation. It perpetuates a recurring pattern in individuals. They experience a lack of self-esteem and motivation, resulting in their inertia and subsequent feelings of dissatisfaction with their lack of action. The repetitive pattern perpetuates itself. Treating this condition can be challenging as individuals experiencing depression-induced lack of motivation may not possess the awareness of their own affliction. It is merely a phenomenon that has overtaken your cognitive faculties. The dearth of drive to improve constitutes a component of the issue. Could you enlighten me on techniques employed to instill motivation in individuals? There is a principle that asserts that action comes before motivation. This concept is intriguing as it challenges conventional notions by foregrounding what may seem inherently retrograde. One might assume that motivation is the precursor to action; individuals typically reflect on their reasons for pursuing a particular endeavor before taking the necessary steps to achieve it. According to this concept, motivation follows action. This implies that one must take action even when lacking motivation.

If an individual is able to comprehend this concept, it has the potential to influence their mindset. The essence of what you are attempting to convey is that the key is not to wait for motivation before taking action, but rather to understand that taking action itself leads to motivation. It may be a concise expression, yet it holds significant value. That statement has the ability to penetrate the cloud of indifference that can be generated by the presence of depressive symptoms.

The Relationship Between Fear and Psychological Well-being

An additional manner in which fear hinders your progress is through its adverse effects on your mental well-being. If you do not actively seek opportunities to expand your horizons and immerse yourself in unfamiliar circumstances, the accumulation of fear may progressively hinder your ability to confront new situations. This is due to the growing apprehension of being unfamiliar with how to navigate unfamiliar circumstances, particularly as a result of habitually declining such opportunities. For instance, if you have persisted within the confines of your comfort zone solely over the previous two years, you may presently harbor trepidation that in the event you were to opt for venturing beyond its borders, you would be overwhelmed by fear and uncertainty and consequently struggle to navigate proficiently. As a result, this prolongs your adherence to your comfort zone, thereby facilitating the perpetuation of fear.

Chronic Fear

Persistent fear can develop into anxiety if one resides under its influence for an extended period of time. Although anxiety may not manifest, the perpetuation of fear within one's body can potentially precipitate a variety of health-related concerns in the future. Several of these problems encompass gastrointestinal issues, a compromised immune system, cognitive decline, and challenges in fear regulation over an extended period. In the event that your brain remains chronically besieged by apprehension, it produces discernible effects on your physique since the physiological responses triggered by fear are inherently designed for transient durations. When these changes endure, owing to the persistence of fear, it can exert a detrimental influence on the physical well-being. If you have ever experienced an overwhelming sense of fear stemming from a distressing encounter, it is probable that you recollect feeling considerable exhaustion in its aftermath. This can be attributed to the fact that fear exerts considerable strain on the human physique. Some of the physiological effects associated with it encompass enhancing the muscular blood flow in areas such as the legs, impeding the digestive process, and dilating the pupils, among various other manifestations. These modifications collectively contribute to an individual's ability to engage in combat or flee; however, when they endure due to phobias such as anticipatory anxiety, they no longer bear positive effects on our well-being.

The Correlation Between Fear and Self-Assurance and Self-Regard

The correlation between fear and low self-confidence arises from a deficiency of self- reliance and faith in one's aptitude to navigate unfamiliar circumstances. If one lacks self-assurance, it is probable that they also lack confidence in their capacities, particularly when it pertains to managing adversity. Each day, we encounter various challenges that necessitate our ability to adapt. Among these trials, confronting unfamiliar and discomforting circumstances is a daunting yet indispensable requirement for personal growth and triumph. A lack of self-assurance leads to a perception of inadequacy in our ability to manage situations proficiently, thereby manifesting as fear. The apprehension of inadequate coping abilities, the concern of appearing foolish in the presence of unfamiliar individuals, or the dread of experiencing a psychological collapse are all potential consequences accompanied by the presence of diminished self-esteem.

Having a strong sense of self-worth enables us to possess the assurance to make sound decisions and effectively navigate unfamiliar and challenging circumstances. We can confront novel circumstances that may provoke trepidation with unwavering assurance in our capacity to overcome them, and potentially acquire valuable insights from these encounters. We are not succumbing to fear, nor allowing it to hinder us from embracing the opportunities that may be intimidating.

Having a diminished sense of self-worth can lead us to perceive ourselves as individuals of inferior value or lacking deservingness. Additionally, this can lead to the apprehension of being surpassed by fear, stemming from our concerns about potential rejection from unfamiliar individuals or in novel circumstances. Consider a scenario such as a initial encounter, in which we are required to step beyond the boundaries of our familiar territory by acquainting ourselves with a new individual, dedicating time to familiarize ourselves with their character, and anticipating that they will find gratification in joining us for this occasion. Individuals with diminished self-confidence may anticipate that their company will hold negative opinions of them, derive limited enjoyment from the social engagement, and ultimately reject any future prospects of furthering their relationship. This induces a sense of apprehension, thereby impeding the individual's willingness to embark on a romantic encounter in the initial phase. Self-esteem and fear exhibit a strong interconnectedness.

Contrarily, individuals possessing a strong sense of self-worth will perceive themselves as inherently likable, attributing a lack of interest in a second date to the other person rather than internalizing it as a reflection of their own shortcomings. An individual characterized by a strong sense of self-worth possesses unwavering confidence in their character, demeanor, and physical presentation. The individuals might experience some anxiety ahead of their initial encounter, but they will not harbor trepidation regarding potential rejection as they possess an inherent sense of self-worth that does not hinge upon seeking validation from others.

Fear arises when individuals who possess diminished self-confidence or low self-esteem encounter circumstances or occurrences that they perceive as demanding or threatening. They lack the capacity to supplant these fear-induced emotions with cognitive reflections on their own competence, highlighting their history of successfully conquering intimidating circumstances. Typically, apprehension serves as a deterrent, discouraging individuals from venturing into such circumstances or encounters when afforded the option, due to their preoccupation with the multitude of potential risks that may materialize if they choose to expose themselves.

Approaching Motivation

There exist numerous inquiries regarding personal motivation or its absence, as well as motivation observed in others. People frequently inquire as to the reasons behind their own or someone else's lack of motivation.

Managers frequently inquire, 'What measures can be implemented to inspire and drive team members?' However, the predicament lies in their quest for a straightforward remedy, such as organizing a team building event, with the expectation that it will produce miraculous outcomes.

They believe that by simply waving a mystical instrument, they will instantaneously acquire motivation. Even with the utilization of the most renowned and esteemed motivational speaker, the likelihood of attaining anything beyond a transient surge of motivation remains improbable.

It typically does not culminate in the team exhibiting greater motivation for collaborative efforts. Why? If a distinct rationale or underlying theme for the individuals within that team is not present, their motivation and productivity will remain stagnant. The aforementioned statement applies to individual motivation as well. Numerous individuals embark on a quest for the elusive formula that bestows motivation, rather than simply clarifying their purpose or rationale.

What are the benefits for me?

We tend to be intrinsically motivated when the fundamental questions are adequately addressed, primarily addressing the significance or purpose behind an action or decision. What is the underlying rationale for me to engage in this activity? What are the benefits or advantages for me? Why does this pertain to me?

In order to foster motivation, there must be an incentivizing factor. Even if you possess the intrinsic drive to assist others, it elicits a profound sense of well-being, granting you a sense of fulfillment and a clear sense of direction. It is essential to develop and possess a valid justification for maintaining consistent and diligent effort. For what other reason would you expend the effort and generally forgo engaging in an activity that you might otherwise derive pleasure from?

Have you ever pondered the rationale behind being required to study certain subjects in school that did not particularly captivate your interest? The most likely answer is "because it is a component of the curriculum." Has this served as a source of motivation and inspiration for you to excel? While it is likely that you complied, as failing to do so may have resulted in negative consequences, it is evident that you did not approach the task with a sense of motivation, enthusiasm, or excitement.

However, I am endeavoring

How effective is it in addressing the circumstances wherein one may be inclined to cease smoking, strive for weight loss, reduce alcohol consumption, or engage in more physical exercise, despite lacking genuine motivation? Have you ever encountered an individual who has been endeavoring to quit smoking? Please respond to a single inquiry: do they engage in smoking or not? The issue lies in the connotation associated with the term attempting.

The term "trying" suggests a lack of genuine motivation or strong commitment, but rather indicates making an effort or attempting something with some degree of intention. Only when one perceives a compelling rationale and makes a conscious decision to take action, will they be sufficiently motivated to modify their habits and attain their desired objectives.

Absence of a definitive resolution and a compelling rationale may exert considerable effort, but the prospects of attaining success remain improbable. No quantity of teambuilding exercises, motivational speakers, or programs can accomplish this for you. No incentives will be effective in fostering motivation beyond mere compliance unless one personally perceives a motive or a valid justification.

The greater the number of motifs, the higher the level of motivation.

Generally speaking, it can be surmised that the greater the number of reasons underlying a particular action, the greater the accompanying benefits, and correspondingly, the higher the likelihood of experiencing increased motivation. Regardless of the numerous justifications provided by others or the extent of their attempts to convince or sway you, unless it aligns with your personal values and what you deem significant, you simply cannot and will not be compelled to take action.

One can lead a horse to water, but one cannot compel it to drink. Ultimately, no external entity possesses the ability to instill motivation within oneself except for the individual themselves. The greater the alignment between your activities and goals with your personal values, the higher the level of motivation you will experience.

It is improbable that you will derive motivation from what is expected of you, as opposed to pursuing activities that you have a genuine passion for. Our motivation is also influenced by what I refer to as 'secondary motivation'.

Secondary motivation refers to the act of being driven to take action due to the potential unfavorable consequences that may arise if one fails to do so.

Failing to achieve weight reduction and neglecting your physical well-being may lead to illness. Similarly, if you neglect to complete your tax return, make your mortgage payments, earn an income, and so forth. There will be associated expenses and physical discomfort; in essence, it can be described as pain.

The greater the number of persuasive justifications one can discover for engaging in a particular action, the higher their level of motivation will be, thus leading to a greater ease in accomplishing tasks. The absence of motivation can be attributed to the absence of distinct primary or secondary advantages.

When experiencing a lack of motivation in areas of one's life that hold significance, it is advisable to scrutinize the "payoff," that is, the underlying reason or benefit for remaining stagnant. Furthermore, it should be noted that one cannot force the horse to drink, but it is possible to induce a significant level of thirst in it!

Am I being lazy?

Numerous individuals mistakenly equate a lack of motivation with laziness. In essence, the concept of laziness is fundamentally non-existent. However, it is possible for motivation to be lacking due to a dearth of incentive. If one desires to examine this hypothesis, they may solicit a teenager to undertake the task of organizing their living space and observe their ensuing reaction.

It is possible that you have erroneously perceived the lack of enthusiasm as laziness. Now kindly request the adolescent to depart from the premises. Conceal currency within various locations in their designated area and challenge them to retrieve as much as possible within a two-minute timeframe. What are your thoughts regarding the potential outcome for the adolescent characterized as 'indolent'?

Rise, emerge, and take decisive action...or choose otherwise.

Motivation is the driving force behind the realization of objectives. It is what facilitates your departure from the current seating arrangement, ceases the introduction of harmful substances into your physical organism, and propels you towards the actualization of your genuine desires in life. Henceforth, refrain from squandering your time by referring to yourself as lazy or partaking in feeble endeavors through mere "trying."

Rather, devote time to discovering your motivation. You will discover that there are certain factors that inspire you and other factors that do not. No individual possesses the authority to dictate what ought to or ought not to serve as your source of motivation. Diverse individuals find motivation from varying sources.

If you experience a sense of compulsion to engage in excessive eating, smoking, drinking, etc. that\'s okay. You are aware of the potential repercussions, and if you opt to acknowledge them, it will be entirely at your discretion. Consequently, take action! The crucial element is to refrain from deceiving oneself. It is evident that you possess the drive and dedication to engage in these activities; otherwise, you would not be actively involved in them.

What limits am I prepared to push?

As previously stated, a facet of my endeavor to secure companionship was in conflict with my personal welfare. I found myself constrained and confined against my will due to the actions of another individual. As I have grown more familiar with myself, an aspect that I hold dear is consistently pushing myself beyond my limits. I am determined to prove to myself that I have the ability to accomplish feats that previously appeared unattainable.

I lacked a platform on which I could express my thoughts and emotions. Currently, within a span of a few months, I have successfully developed and orchestrated the creation of my personal website, enabling me to exercise full authority over its content. The establishment of my personal online domain has indeed exemplified my ability to allocate significant resources towards my top priorities and successfully bring them to completion.

I am utterly indifferent to the opinions of those in my social circle regarding my unconventional preferences. I am indifferent to whether they perceive positive reasoning as futile. I would welcome their examination of my current state, as it would allow them to observe the noticeable transformation I have undergone since my time in high school or college. I wholeheartedly cherish the opportunity to disseminate my experiences, and when individuals reach out to express that my content has positively impacted them, there is absolutely no other sensation that surpasses it.

I showcased to myself the transcendence of boundaries through engaging in conversations with my acquaintances regarding the power of optimistic thinking. I personally acknowledged that it is possible for me to openly showcase my interests to the public while still deeming them praiseworthy and remarkable, regardless of others' opinions. I have proven to myself that I possess a deep level of genuine concern for the aspects that define my unique identity. Additionally, it evokes a heightened sensation.

I perpetually engage in self-inquiry.

I love asking myself newer inquiries. The reason behind this is my earnest desire to comprehend change. Engaging in activities based on the preferences of others can be likened to relinquishing control of one's actions. Do you not need to consider the worthiness of something based on the endorsement of individuals whom you hold in high regard, thus implying that it is worthy of gratitude? Certainly not. Absolutely not. Under no circumstances.

The quote that I particularly favor is attributed to Earl Nightingale, which states, "Inconsistency, as opposed to fortitude, should not be considered a weakness but rather a state of congruity."

By posing self-inquiries such as "what is the enduring impression I wish to leave on others after 80 years" or "how does a typical day unfold for me," I am compelling myself to envision and plan for the future. What modifications do I presently need to enact to ensure the attainment of the desired future in my later years?

Through consistently posing inquiries to myself, I believe I am in a privileged position to uncover minute details that I can modify in order to secure a prosperous future for myself. This could encompass a range of actions, such as embarking on a particular engagement and encountering an individual, going out of my way to visit my acquaintance, allocating an additional 5 minutes for personal needs during the week, or ensuring that I consistently rise at 7 a.m. daily. Although these progressions may not be exceptional, their impact does not rely on being extraordinary.

What is the appropriate manner in which to interact with others?

I have consciously made the proactive choice to prioritize my intrinsic happiness above any form of praise or criticism that may come my way. Is it typical for this one to go flawlessly? No, obviously not. Truthfully, from my perspective, this particular item is the most challenging among the entire compilation. Nonetheless, once I attain it, it brings me unparalleled gratification. This serves as an indicator of my intrinsic self-esteem, as it reaffirms that the worth I assign to myself is solely derived from my own thoughts and evaluations, rather than being reliant on the opinions of others.

How should one manage their solitude?

While I am riding this genuine train, I will simply state here that this one is the least demanding for me. Nevertheless, after engaging in conversations with numerous individuals and thoroughly examining a vast number of articles, it has become evident that this aspect tends to pose the greatest challenge for individuals.

By attentively listening to your contemplations alone, you genuinely cultivate a profound sense of self. By virtue of this sense of self, I possessed the capability to attract affectionate, considerate individuals into my life who were drawn to me based on the energy I emanated. Nevertheless, I would not have had the opportunity to engage in any of these endeavors had I not endured a remarkably challenging and enlightening period of independence.

When I sense the overwhelming influence of life, my usual course of action is to withdraw from social interactions. It represents the most convenient method for me to engage with my emotions. I perform any of the aforementioned tasks in isolation and start to experience a sense of being established. I do not experience terror from my musings, rather, I actively embrace them. I acknowledge and validate my emotions, and I proceed to engage in introspection and self-improvement in order to realign myself with the desired state.

I surmise that numerous individuals may be hesitant to engage in introspection due to the potential repercussions of confronting unfavorable aspects of oneself. That truly is disgusting. I strongly believe that I was in a significantly disadvantaged position, however, upon thorough introspection, I discovered no evidence or justification to support this belief. However, the reason that should compel you to overcome that fear is as follows: You have no intentions of departing from your own company anytime soon, thus it would be wise to foster an appreciation for the person you have become. Your associates are free to depart at their own discretion. It is imperative to devote an equal, if not greater, degree of energy and commitment to individuals who remain until the conclusion.

Am I willing to acknowledge my mistakes?

Finding solace within oneself entails embracing one's imperfections and acknowledging one's fallibility as a mere human prone to making mistakes.

Henceforth, you can bestow upon those individuals whom you have inflicted harm upon something of utmost importance - a sense of conclusion. When you possess an ample amount of self-esteem and engage in sincere self-reflection, you can abstain from inadvertently causing harm to those whom you hold dear. You do not employ false facades, deceit, or suppress emotions in order to safeguard your misinformed perception of self.

When you demonstrate self-love by offering an apology, you afford solace to those who require it.

You exhibit signs of fecklessness by failing to extend enough self-affection to express remorse. I acknowledge that this constitutes a direct link to one's sense of value, as it demonstrates the extent to which an individual can be authentic with themselves. If one finds it necessary to engage in self-deception regarding one's true emotions, it is probable that a significant disconnect exists between oneself and one's feelings. There have been multiple instances wherein I have come to the realization of my incorrectness, yet I was unable to apologize due to my excessive obstinacy and the subsequent embarrassment of being in the wrong. Having stumbled upon the correlation between self-esteem and forgiveness, I have come to comprehend that it constitutes a conclusive reflection of my being, indicating the extent to which I nurture self-affection.

Comparisons

I started university. I had an immense anticipation for it. So many possibilities. Engaging in social interactions, engaging in football activities, and experiencing the lifestyle in a different urban center... Sheffield.

I participated in the freshers' week festivities in 2009 and thoroughly enjoyed the experience.

My drinking and partying with friends at home had given me some practice.

Additionally, it is advisable to invest your efforts into developing socially-oriented proficiencies rather than focusing on enhancing drinking skills.

In contrast, I discovered that during my initial few weeks, the male individuals in my vicinity engaged in the act of socializing with females and subsequently accompanying them back to their respective dwellings. These individuals appeared to be highly renowned. I was lacking the necessary self-assurance to engage in conversation with the girls. What approach did I take in this matter?

Rather than allocating more effort towards self-improvement, I began endeavoring to emulate the sartorial styles of these gentlemen. I possessed average physical appearance, yet I lacked adequate knowledge and understanding in attempting to emulate their distinct styles.

Gradually, my self-esteem began to deteriorate.

I transitioned from my previous self due to a lack of self-acceptance.

In addition, there existed an athlete by the name of Adam.

Adam was a proficient athlete who consistently engaged in an enduring pursuit of running. His coach provided positive affirmation, acknowledging his commendable performance. He derived a sense of satisfaction from this outcome initially, however, his confidence wavered as he observed individuals of his same age achieving significantly superior timings.

He would consistently show up for his running sessions, however, his enthusiasm gradually waned.

When engaging in self-comparisons, we relinquish control over external factors.

When we shift our attention away from ourselves, we consequently divert our focus from the essence of our identity.

Hence, our attention must be directed towards ourselves.

Enjoy improving yourself. Enjoy trying your best.

Take pleasure in engaging in activities that align with your interests and contribute to your sense of self. All of these elements are within your jurisdiction.

In a subsequent chapter, I delve into the utilization of a role model as a means to cultivate confidence. It can be advantageous to adopt positive qualities, but refrain from attempting to emulate others. Embrace your individuality, for others have already claimed their own identities.

The paramount message I would like to emphasize regarding comparisons, as well as other facets delineated in the book, is the significant concept of self-acceptance. In order to initiate progress, it is essential to acknowledge and embrace one's current circumstances. It entails acknowledging and valuing your current circumstances, while actively striving towards personal growth. When we evade or escape from our unique circumstances, we are conveying to ourselves the implicit notion that we hold a negative opinion of our own selves. We aspire to emulate someone else. What impact do you believe this has on our self-esteem?

Action:

Record your daily accomplishments in a journal. Simply taking note of 3-5 accomplishments that I successfully complete on a daily basis greatly enhances my emotional state and instills a sense of pride in my achievements. There is no necessity for you to engage in substantial endeavors. Examples of such activities could include engaging in physical exercise such as attending a fitness center, taking a lengthy stroll, contributing substantively during a meeting, or various other actions that yield positive implications.

Instances of accomplishments to be documented within a journal entry following a day:

- An enjoyable stroll

- Giving praise to someone else

- Engaging in meaningful dialogue with an individual

- Participating in fitness activities at the gym

- Participating in a sports team practice session

- Tackling a challenging task in the workplace
- Engaging in a complex task in the professional setting
- Undertaking a demanding assignment during work hours
- Taking on a difficult task in the context of one's employment

- Contemplative practice

Engaging in speech rehearsal

- Writing in a diary or journal

- Accomplishing a domestic responsibility that has been postponed.
- Attaining completion of a household duty that has been procrastinated.
- Fulfilling a pending assignment related to one's residence.

An recommended exercise is the process of integrating and ingraining novel beliefs within one's framework. The reason behind our tendency to make comparisons with others stems from our lack of self-assurance in our own capabilities. The utilization of the affirmative statement "I am sufficient, I am exceptional" has greatly facilitated my journey towards self-acceptance and self-appreciation.

I express it a minimum of three times daily, allocating a few minutes to each instance.

It subliminally infiltrates my subconscious. Thus, articulating this notion to oneself can yield substantial advantages. It may not yield immediate outcomes; however, over time, you will gradually develop faith in it and perceive its effects. What potential losses do you perceive in this situation? Adopting a different mindset requires a minimal exertion of energy.

Perpetual Self-Enhancement Is The Key To Success

Thus, it is evident that you have experienced a notable enhancement in your self-confidence. You have successfully progressed and evolved through the implementation of your affirmations. Should you have availed yourself of therapeutic services, engaged in enhancing your positive mindset, I now propose that it is opportune to acquire further insights on sustaining this personal development.

Maintaining a positive mindset and cultivating a positive outlook are decisions that need to be made on a daily basis. It is not an immediate occurrence, nor does it transpire without consistent determination. Developing one's self-esteem and pursuing personal growth should not be regarded as an innate talent or ability. It is a choice.

The objective at present shifts to gradually constructing and cultivating your self-esteem from the ground up. Your objective entails continual growth, fostering a positive mindset, and expressing gratitude. The greater your positivity, the more your self-esteem will flourish.

Keep Growing

To ensure the progression of one's self-esteem and facilitate personal development, it is imperative to continuously cultivate growth and advancement. The development should occur in relation to assuming accountability for oneself, one's identity, and one's actions. As one cultivates an increasing sense of self-worth, they concurrently bolster their inner assurance, fortitude, and principles.

You are currently seeking personal development. You are eager to dedicate yourself to continuous personal development, aimed at enhancing your self-assurance. This is an objective that requires daily commitment on your part. We may encounter obstacles and deviations along the path, but rest assured, you are gradually progressing towards becoming the individual you aspire to be and are capable of becoming.

Some of the methods to foster continuous growth include:

• Acknowledge your areas of proficiency and areas in need of improvement, and strive to achieve a harmonious equilibrium in your life.

- Enabling the positive enhancements you have experienced in your self-esteem and self-confidence to pave the way for your progression and unlock new opportunities, ensuring your continuous personal growth.

- Always keep in mind that personal growth and development are of utmost importance in the trajectory of your life.

- The greater one's self-awareness, the more one possesses the potential to cultivate their self-esteem.

Do not become overly concerned with inconsequential matters...they are all trivial matters.

In the year 1997, the renowned author Richard Carlson penned the book titled 'Don't Sweat the Small Stuff ... It's all Small Stuff'. In this publication, Carlson observed the multitude of individuals bustling about and experiencing heightened levels of anxiety. He harbored the belief that a great number of individuals devoted their lives to futile anxiety. He had a tendency to assert that traffic remained oblivious to and unconcerned about one's emotional state of stress.

Instead of succumbing to stress, endeavor to cultivate a mindset of gratitude. It is important to bear in mind the significance of displaying gratitude on a daily basis. This practice of displaying gratitude shall enable you to attain the competence to alleviate any stress you may experience, particularly stress pertaining to trivial matters.

It is permissible to experience fear - Engage in the task you believe to be impossible.

Eleanor Roosevelt, in articulating her aspirations for women to seize greater agency in their lives, aid society, and demand parity with men, asserted: "When confronted with fear, one must undertake that which they deem impossible."

Endeavor to accomplish that which you believe to be beyond your capabilities. Confront the task that evokes the greatest apprehension within you, the one that appears insurmountable. Have courage. It elicits a far greater sense of exhilaration than that of fear. Courage according to Mrs. Roosevelt offers a greater source of excitement than fear, ultimately making it more straightforward in the grand scheme of things. Roosevelt delivered a speech prior to the onset of the Second World War, urging individuals to rid themselves of fear. As you experience a greater number of life's challenges, you will develop an enhanced ability to overcome them.

For Mrs. Concerning individuals endeavoring to enhance their self-esteem, the true peril lies in passivity, in evading the confrontation of one's fears. Individuals who possess diminished self-esteem may find it challenging to confront their fears due to the apprehension that failure may result in a further decline in their self-assurance. Consequently, it is imperative that you achieve success with every endeavor. It is imperative that you undertake the task which you perceive to be beyond your abilities.

Learn from your Mistakes

The concluding aspect of this fifth step pertaining to the process of perpetual self-improvement involves acquiring knowledge from the errors committed. Given your significant personal growth resulting from the diligent efforts you have invested in enhancing your self-confidence, you are now capable of undertaking this task without further delay.

You have the opportunity to learn from mistakes, regardless of their magnitude. Allocate sufficient time for a comprehensive analysis of the preceding events, your actions, and potential alternatives that could yield a dissimilar result. This is not merely about rectifying your error, but rather about cultivating an ability to avoid committing the same misstep in the future, and altering your approach based on the lessons gleaned from this mistake.

The Behaviors of an Optimistic Individual

Individuals who adopt an optimistic mindset and exhibit positive attributes typically adhere to a discernible pattern of behaviors and preferences. Their lifestyles exhibit a discernible pattern, albeit one that is not unfavorable. When you interact with an individual who possesses a positive mindset, you are likely to observe the manifestation of these behaviors on numerous occasions. If one aspires to cultivate a mindset of optimism, it is likely that they would desire to adopt these practices in their own behavior.

These habits that we are about to acquaint you with are those that will aid you in cultivating a positive mindset. They will aid you in developing improved interactions with your surrounding environment. They will assist you in aligning your lifestyle to create an environment conducive to the natural influx of positivity. Keep in mind, the cultivation of positivity is possible, but it can also be magnetically drawn towards us. These habits can assist in the adoption of commonly observed behaviors that promote a positive mindset.

It is permissible if significant time and effort are required to firmly establish these favorable aspects for oneself. If it is necessary for you to regulate your speed, it would be advisable to do so. By attempting to execute all the tasks simultaneously and becoming inundated, you may potentially experience a decrease in your willingness to endure all the responsibilities. Rather, strive to gradually embrace those positive habits in your life.

Promoting Optimal Well-being through Healthy Living

Maintaining a healthy way of life is crucial for fostering a positive outlook. It is imperative that you ensure the soundness of your lifestyle. Extensive evidence suggests that individuals who engage in regular physical activity exhibit notably higher levels of positivity. Typically, individuals experience an improvement in their self-perception and a heightened sense of confidence, as engaging in physical exercise triggers the release of mood-enhancing hormones, resulting in an overall sense of well-being. It will assist in fostering a sense of purpose and joy that holds significance to them. Engaging in physical activity is beneficial for one's well-being, and it is imperative to make it an indispensable part of your lifestyle, irrespective of personal inclination or preference.

Accepting Rejection

Individuals with a positive mindset possess the ability to gracefully embrace rejection. Similar to the case of failure, they possess the ability to recognize and take into account instances of mishap, typically demonstrating the capacity to embrace and come to terms with the outcome. In the event of a denied application, individuals may experience emotional distress or dissatisfaction, yet they have the ability to acknowledge the outcome without feeling obligated to contest or seek a review of the decision. They possess the capacity to acknowledge the possibility of failure, despite exerting their utmost efforts, without allowing it to divert their focus from their priorities.

Adopting an optimistic mindset

The importance of maintaining a positive mindset holds great significance, and throughout this entire book, we have consistently emphasized and advocated for this perspective. Your thoughts hold significance as well, and thus, considering the impact of the words that you use to express your true beliefs, it is imperative to ensure that your thoughts are imbued with positivity rather than any alternative perspective. If deliberation is necessary, it is imperative to construct thoughts using positive language, ensuring the potential of achieving the desired outcome that one seeks. By acquiring the skill of utilizing positive language, one can generally discern the exact message and appropriate timing for communication.

Replacing "Have" with "Acquire"

An additional illustration pertains to the employment of affirmative language and utilizing language as a means to regulate one's cognition, constituting a mere marginal adjustment. Whenever possible, refrain from utilizing the term "Have" when expressing a sense of obligation. Rather than being obligated to do something, frame it as being afforded the opportunity to do something. This minor adjustment will, in fact, yield significant and far-reaching consequences if incorporated into your routine on a consistent basis. By simply altering the manner in which you communicate with yourself, you will observe a shift in your overall disposition.

Avoiding Complaining

Optimistic individuals also strive to refrain from making complaints. Adverse outcomes are possible; however, rather than lamenting deviations from the intended course, it is more prudent to invest efforts in exploring alternative approaches to resolve the issue. Rather than becoming trapped by your current obligations or succumbing to disappointment, it is more advisable to explore alternative approaches for future endeavors. Rather than becoming entangled in continuous complaints or expressing dissatisfaction, which will have limited impact aside from possibly providing temporary emotional release, it would be advisable to pause and contemplate potential solutions for the future. What measures can be taken to address the issue at hand? What actions can be taken to determine a viable solution instead?

By refraining from complaining, you allocate your mental resources towards problem-solving. Expressing grievances is merely a psychological burden, and it is more advantageous to completely eradicate this practice rather than persistently yielding to it. Although venting may provide temporary solace, it is crucial to consider whether it truly contributes to your personal advancement in any meaningful way. If not, refrain from expressing complaints.

Direct your attention to the current conflict at hand.

Frequently, there is a strong temptation to incorporate past interactions into a fresh dispute. You and the other individual are engaged in a disagreement regarding the potential purchase of a new item, when unexpectedly, a fortuitous development occurs. Do you recall that moment when you failed to address (mention unrelated issue)? Abruptly, the conversation veers towards an unanticipated topic, wherein both parties delve into a prolonged discussion about an unrelated matter, unrelated to the original argument of the day.

When we persist in clinging to the past, our capacity to make sound, logical choices diminishes. Instead of seeking resolution for the current conflict, we delve into historical investigations in order to uncover information that might aid in one's victory in the debate or silence the opponent.

Display a readiness to release and relinquish

Releasing can be a highly intricate task, as it frequently involves grappling with internal conflict regarding whether one is truly relinquishing control or merely suppressing the matter.

It is imperative to recognize that it is necessary for you to address and resolve the issue prior to contemplating the possibility of releasing it. It is imperative that you reach a point where you can unequivocally respond in the negative when examining whether the issue still vexes you.

When one chooses to conceal unresolved matters, the potential for continued distress remains and merely constitutes a delay in addressing them. Therefore, when making the decision to release, it is advisable to choose a moment in which you are experiencing lower levels of anger, stress, and volatility. This will enable you to objectively evaluate the consequences of your decision. If you continue to experience difficulty in relinquishing attachment, it is possible that the matter has not been adequately addressed.

Choose your conflicts.

Not all potential conflicts will require your input. As you develop a heightened sense of emotional awareness, you will be empowered to discern the endeavors that warrant your dedication and those that do not.

Conflicts constitute high-pressure circumstances which can significantly deplete your energy. Therefore, it is imperative to selectively involve oneself in conflicts that have the potential to enhance one's perspective, overall well-being, and foster a greater level of comprehension.

Relationship/Social Awareness

How can one determine the authenticity of someone's intentions when they employ indirect communication? How do you effectively engage with someone who is resistant to opening up?

To attain emotional intelligence and evolve from the experiences you have encountered, it is imperative to redirect your comprehension of your own emotional state towards comprehending the emotional disposition of the other individual.

Social consciousness is what enables us to cultivate and sustain interpersonal connections.

By prioritizing the comprehension of the other individual beyond their verbal communication, you can achieve a more comprehensive understanding of them. Consequently, what measures can be taken to cultivate social consciousness?

Listen Keenly

Active listening is a crucial skill that is rarely perfected, despite its significance. It is tough to listen, especially when you also have issues of your own going on. To establish effective interpersonal connections, or enhance them, one must engage in active listening.

Engaging in active listening enables one to perceive and comprehend the perspective of others, gaining insight into their unique worldview. Engaging in attentive listening, whereby one restates the speaker's words soon after they have been expressed, enables the establishment of a meaningful bond with the interlocutor.

By actively engaging in attentive listening, you have the ability to empathize with the viewpoint of others, thereby enhancing your comprehension of them.

Exercise awareness of non-verbal signals

Psychologists assert that non-verbal communication often conveys a greater amount of information than verbal communication. However, let us refrain from overly concentrating on the veracity of this claim and instead consider a scenario in which we find ourselves disinclined to vocalize our thoughts and emotions. What are your usual activities?

In the event that you are situated in a crowded environment while awaiting someone, it is possible that you may unconsciously engage in a behavior characterized by the repetitive tapping motion of an object, such as a table or the armrest of your chair, as a manifestation of impatience. Alternatively, when afflicted by feelings of anxiety and restlessness, you may resort to engaging in repetitive manipulation of objects within your grasp.

Frequently, these signals are transmitted unconsciously on certain occasions. Hence, even when we express thoughts that are incongruent with our emotional state, our physical gestures and demeanor can potentially reveal the truth.

Embark On Your Quest For Self-Discovery Starting Today

Your endeavor to enhance your own self will be challenging. It will present numerous challenges and expose you to various circumstances that will continually prompt you to question your sense of self-value. Do not allow fear to inhibit you, as ultimately, you shall attain a heightened sense of self-awareness.

Self-regard and self-assurance are cultivated through persistent application and a substantial amount of exertion. It will test your patience, exposing you to numerous instances of trial and error. It is imperative for one to acknowledge that the concept of flawless self-esteem does not exist. Individuals who possess unwavering self-assurance are cognizant of the possibility of failure, acknowledging its inevitability. Embrace this aspect of your being; even more so, embrace your complete self - acknowledging that you are akin to all individuals, with both virtues and flaws. It is crucial to alter one's mindset and transition from perceiving oneself as inadequate to recognizing the abundant untapped potential within.

It constitutes a considerable undertaking, one characterized by considerable difficulty. There will inevitably be moments in which you may stumble and encounter disappointment, yet it is through such challenges that you shall garner the invaluable lessons shaping your resilience. As you engage in a deliberate endeavor to enhance your personal growth, you will develop a heightened sense of self-awareness regarding your experiences. With the insights conveyed within the pages of this book, you will acquire the necessary tools to confront your personal challenges, the resourcefulness to persist, and the determination to sustain your pursuit in the quest for self-improvement.

Amidst the adversities one encounters, it is essential to consistently acknowledge and embrace the minor yet meaningful moments of positivity. Please make a conscious effort to acknowledge your small successes and use them as stepping stones for further progress. Use them to propel yourself to become better. These small yet extraordinary manifestations of brilliance should be treasured and regarded with great value. These benefits are a direct result of your personal exertion and steadfast determination. When faced with a somber and desolate environment, reflect upon the instances of positivity encountered throughout your journey and allow those luminous occasions to serve as your guiding light.

We sincerely trust that this book has provided you with valuable perspectives on cultivating your self-esteem and confidence as an individual, transcending gender distinctions. The global community eagerly anticipates your arrival and will undoubtedly be enriched by your existence. Eventually, you will reflect upon this voyage of self-exploration and personal growth with a joyful countenance and a subdued assurance to declare, "I have accomplished it!"

Chapter 8: Notable Obstacles to Establishing Self-Assurance

While confidence barriers may vary across individuals due to their unique personal circumstances, experiences, and perspectives, there are commonly encountered barriers that affect everyone. Presented below are five examples:

Fear

The prevailing barrier to maintaining a state of self-assurance is typically rooted in fear. It is possible that you experience apprehension towards failure, aversion to rejection, or even anxiety regarding achieving success. One might experience apprehension towards achieving success due to the elevated standards, heightened expectations, and increased responsibilities that accompany it. Nevertheless, the overwhelming majority of your apprehensions are unfounded. These fears are only present within the confines of your own consciousness. Please take a moment to reflect upon the concerns that erode your self-assurance. Do they possess a solid foundation in any factual basis? Is there any substantiation to suggest their eventual realization? Do you possess apprehension towards a hypothetical scenario or an improbable occurrence? Furthermore, in the event that any aspect of your apprehension materializes, it is seldom as daunting or incapacitating as you anticipate it to be.

Worry and Overthinking

An additional hindrance to gaining confidence is the presence of apprehension and repetitive thought patterns. One may persistently harbor concerns about maintaining an impeccable image, the opinions held by others, or the possibility of committing an error or facing failure. Anxiety has the potential to take on a cyclical nature, with repetitive thoughts reinforced through mindless repetition. The human mind tends to cling to a particular thought, much like a gerbil persistently running on its wheel, making it challenging to release.

Anxiety and excessive contemplation arise from possessing a mindset excessively fixated on appearances and superficial consequences, rather than prioritizing self-authenticity, embracing the present moment, and cultivating self-acceptance. Engrossing oneself in purposeful activities, be it professional or recreational, and engaging in acts of service towards others, precludes the indulgence of worries. Your cognitive abilities are currently preoccupied with matters of greater significance. In instances of having spare time and encountering the cycle of worry once more, simply verbalize the term "cease" aloud to disrupt the worrisome thoughts. Subsequently, shift your thoughts towards a more constructive perspective, or occupy your mental faculties by immersing yourself in activities such as literature, penning down written content, offering assistance to others, or fostering creativity.

Procrastination

Procrastination undermines one's self-assurance as it covertly restrains individuals from realizing their full capabilities and hinder them from leading a fulfilling life. Failure to complete tasks or procrastinating detrimentally impacts one's performance, thereby preventing them from achieving their maximum potential. The result will never exhibit the same level of assurance or efficacy. The act of delaying tasks may lead to a sense of inadequacy, yet the solution lies simply in taking the first step. Commencing a task is indisputably the most arduous aspect, necessitating one to seize the initiative.

Establish your priorities, allocate ample time to yourself, and organize your tasks based on your personal preferences. If you frequently encounter the tendency to consistently prioritize a responsibility towards the end, ensure to deliberately elevate that task to the forefront and promptly execute it. Continuing to postpone it will only result in further depletion of your emotional energy. Commence by initiating, undertaking a single minor step, and it will propel you forward until the conclusion—enhancing your assurance in your capacity to undertake future actions.

Indecision

The ability to make decisions, even when you aren't 100 percent sure, is essential for building confidence. Uncertainty has the capacity to immobilize individuals, leaving them ineffectual and plagued by feelings of insecurity. One can effect change by setting self-imposed deadlines for making decisions and firmly adhering to them. Decisions rarely come with a guarantee, so you will always feel some risk with any choice. The task at hand is becoming accustomed to the uneasiness that arises from the absence of certainty. Most choices aren\'t permanent. If new information arises that warrants an adjustment, you have the option to modify your initial decision.

However, delaying the decision until all conditions are optimal can impede your progress. The opportune moment will never present itself, hence it is advisable to choose a rational time and adhere to it. It is more conducive to bolstering one's confidence to come to a decision, even if ultimately proven erroneous, rather than abstaining from decisions altogether. (I will discuss the topic of decision-making in more detail in subsequent chapters.)

Doubt

Doubt frequently serves as the elusive instigator for all the remaining four barriers. The source of your apprehension, anxious thoughts, and inability to make decisions stems from a lack of certainty in your capabilities, discernment, and sound judgment. If one lacks faith in oneself, why should others bestow their belief?

If you possess a track record of engaging in suboptimal choices or exercising flawed discretion, it would be prudent to reflect upon the lessons derived from these occurrences and contemplate ways in which you can effect positive changes moving ahead. Frequently, this is not the situation. As mature individuals, we possess an ample amount of life experience that bestows upon us the qualities of sagacity and discriminative judgment. We possess solely a lack of trust in our own abilities.

Few can rival your inherent understanding of what truly benefits you the most. Embark upon the process of perceiving oneself as an individual endowed with innate wisdom and profound self-awareness. You possess the solutions within your being, even in the absence of confidence in those solutions. One can counter doubt through the cultivation of self-trust by engaging in small actions. Select a situation that is within your capacity and in which you experience uncertainty or lack confidence in your own abilities. Subsequently, exercise your discretion based on careful assessment, notwithstanding any reservations you may have. Engage in the act of executing tasks even in times of uncertainty. Engaging in this activity will enhance your self-assurance.

These prevalent obstacles to self-assurance affect individuals universally. On occasion, each of us encounters feelings of apprehension, concern, delaying action, hesitation, and uncertainty. However, when these emotions become overpowering, hindering our capacity to attain success, foster meaningful connections, express ourselves assertively, or generate a financial income, they must be acknowledged and resolved.

Chapter Three: The Role of Confidence in Observational Skills

I would like to propose that you engage in the practice of observing others, as it can potentially provide you with valuable insights into the possible reasons behind your confidence deficit.

- I am significantly overweight. • I have excessive weight. • I possess an unhealthy amount of body fat. • I am overly obese. • I have an excessive body mass index.

- I am not aesthetically pleasing.

- I do not possess the necessary qualifications or skills to meet the requirements.

- I do not possess sufficient height.

- I am dissatisfied with my choice of attire.

Naturally, the emotions described above extend beyond the superficial remarks provided earlier, yet you possess notions regarding your position within the grand design. You perceive others as possessing greater physical attractiveness, slenderness, superiority relative to yourself, taller stature, or who exhibit a significantly more refined sense of fashion than you do. All these disparaging remarks regarding your character undermine your self-assurance. The point I wish to convey to you is that one's physical appearance, weight, abilities, height, or choice of attire hold no significance. Individuals of various body types exhibit self-assurance; thus, refrain from attributing your limitations and instead, attentively observe those in your vicinity. For the purpose of this activity, kindly proceed to the shopping center or choose an open-air establishment, such as a café, and engage in a diligent observation of individuals.

In your observation, who would you consider to be the individual displaying the highest level of confidence? What set this individual apart from the others? It is a truth that individuals with various body types and sizes demonstrate their confidence through their gait and manner of entering a space. You perceive them exhibiting signs of contentment, with a notable absence of clumsiness or a subdued demeanor. They will confront the world directly and display confident posture. They exhibit no reluctance when approaching individuals. The individual I encountered who exuded the utmost confidence was a woman whose weight surpassed mine by twofold, an impressive feat in itself. Furthermore, she exhibited unwavering contentment with her own self, undoubtedly admirable. It is essential to comprehend that an individual who lacks the ability to see, such as a blind individual, can exude an air of self-assurance solely by virtue of their inner contentment, regardless of their physical appearance. Confidence starts inside you. It is imperative for you to grant approval unto yourself.

After carefully observing individuals, acquaint yourself with their mannerisms upon entering a room, paying close attention to discern the contrasting behaviors exhibited by those who possess confidence and those who do not. Individuals who possess a strong sense of self-assurance emanate a radiant aura that sets them apart from those burdened by self-consciousness. They do not harbor insecurities regarding their physical dimensions and instead exhibit a confident demeanor. The issue at hand pertains to the fact that contemporary society has imposed particular expectations onto your schedule. One can observe flawless models featured in catalogs. You observe individuals who consistently appear to experience a greater degree of fortune than yourself or individuals who exude a sense of happiness and satisfaction in their lives. Allow me to present you with an undeniable reality. If you fail to alter your approach, you will fail to attract individuals into your life who possess the qualities necessary for your happiness. The principle of the Law of Attraction is based on the concept of vibrations, where individuals who possess negative thoughts and low self-awareness emit unfavorable vibrations, subsequently attracting additional negative vibrations. Certainly, it is possible for an individual to exhibit kindness towards you, but would you prefer their kindness to stem from a sense of pity? Would it not be more advantageous if they harbored sincere positive feelings towards you based on their genuine liking for you? When one elevates their standards and cultivates a positive demeanor, they have the ability to make numerous errors without diminishing the affection and regard bestowed upon them by others.

Dressing to kill

It is evident through observation that individuals' level of success and self-confidence is greatly influenced by the manner in which they present themselves to society. You observed it. Therefore, let us examine the contents of your wardrobe and determine which garments provide you with feelings of happiness and comfort. Wearing garments that are ill-fitting due to concerns about the visibility of oversized attire labels is regrettably counterproductive for one's personal benefit. If it holds significant importance for you, I suggest having yourself professionally fitted for undergarments, and if necessary, discreetly remove the size indication label from the underwear. Women who choose to don an ill-fitting brassiere will perpetually experience discomfort and project an appearance of unease. They exhibit protrusions in places where protrusions are unconventional. Likewise, individuals of the male gender who don attire unsuitably styled trousers or pants appear incongruous in their appearance.

The possession of an appropriately proportioned waistline contributes to an increased level of personal comfort, as it alleviates the need for constant adjustments and minimizes self-consciousness. Therefore, adopt a strategy of starting with the foundational elements of your attire and ensure that each article of clothing enhances your self-assurance.

Proceed into your bedroom and approach the full-length mirror. In the attire that you have carefully selected, kindly present yourself and express introspective thoughts on this ensemble that imbues you with a sense of self-assurance. Clothes are not you. Nonetheless, they do play a role in shaping initial perceptions, and if one lacks self-assurance, presenting oneself in a well-groomed manner can significantly enhance one's prospects. Ensuring that one's appearance is presentable, with neatly combed hair, a clean face, and well-maintained hands, conveys a sense of self-care and can contribute positively to others' perceptions. Engaging in habits such as nail-biting, sporting unclean footwear, and neglecting personal grooming can lead others to perceive you as lacking self-assurance, upon their initial interaction with you. A lack of confidence does not contribute positively to one's self-perception. Consequently, one's outward appearance carries significance. If one were to deliver a speech while donning trousers with a constrictive waistline and footwear that induces instability, it would serve to capture the attention of individuals and elicit observation. Subsequently, you become aware of the disapproving gazes directed towards you, leading to the internalization of negative thoughts that undermine your self-esteem. By endeavoring to address any visual concerns that others may possess regarding your appearance, you enhance your likelihood of projecting an image of confidence and adeptness in presenting yourself in a manner that conforms to societal expectations.

When Is It Appropriate To Exhibit Extroverted Behaviors?

There are occasions when it may be necessary to adopt an extraverted disposition in order to accomplish specific objectives. It is advisable to engage in this practice when undertaking projects of personal significance or those intended for individuals who hold a special place in your life. Nevertheless, it is imperative to take into account certain principles to prevent undue strain when assuming an extroverted demeanor.

Please ascertain the project that requires your attention.

Initially, it is imperative to consider the project that requires your attention. It is imperative to ascertain the initial and concluding stages of the project. It is imperative to also ascertain the requisite actions that must be undertaken in order to achieve project completion.

Acquire the necessary aptitudes

The subsequent step you must undertake involves the identification of the extravert skills that necessitate usage. You might be obligated to interact with unfamiliar individuals or engage in marketing activities whereas potential customers are concerned. If you are involved in the realm of personnel management, it may be necessary for you to assume a leadership role to guide individuals throughout the duration of the project.

In certain instances, you may be required to exhibit a greater degree of sociability. You will be required to interact with additional individuals. There are occasions when it becomes necessary to host individuals with whom one has limited acquaintance. These activities are not typically aligned with introverted tendencies, yet it is necessary to engage in them for significant undertakings.

Assign tasks that are delegable

If you are in a leadership position, you may want to delegate extravert tasks to true extraverts who are more qualified to do the task based on their personality. It is important for you to recognize that certain responsibilities do not necessarily require your personal attention.

If the circumstances warrant, undertake the tasks that require extraverted qualities on your own. There may be instances when there is a lack of proficient extraverts available to handle the assignment on your behalf. There may also arise occasions when the tasks are deemed too crucial to be entrusted to others.

Ensure that the duration of the experience is brief.

In endeavors that require the display of extroverted qualities, it is advisable to commence promptly in order to expedite project completion. We experience increased fatigue when we are compelled to assume a persona that does not align with our authentic identity. We attain awareness of every undertaking. Occasionally, one may experience a sense of discomfort. The perpetual contemplation of our actions can exert a burden on the psyche. If you are a novice in engaging in extraverted activities, it would be advisable to complete them promptly in order to mitigate potential mental exhaustion.

Develop the ability to engage in extroverted behavior that is necessary for regular use.

There exist certain skills of an extraverted nature that we are required to employ on a regular basis for the execution of our professional duties. As an illustration, in the sales field, it is imperative to consistently engage with unfamiliar individuals in order to acquire potential sales opportunities. As a legal professional, it is imperative to regularly engage in client meetings, necessitating frequent outings.

Discern extroverted responsibilities that warrant cultivation to thrive in your professional trajectory. It would be beneficial for you to allocate some time towards practicing the aforementioned skill. Introverted individuals often employ the practice of rehearsing their speeches prior to delivering them. You are welcome to do likewise. In the realm of sales, it is customary for companies to have prearranged scripts readily available for their representatives to articulate during the process of promoting a merchandise. There is no need for you to veer away from this script when you are in the early stages. As you engage in deliberate practice of the skill, your proficiency will progressively enhance, lending a heightened aura of authenticity to your actions. With regular and diligent practice, any skill can rapidly become ingrained and intuitive.

Please make sure to allocate some time for relaxation and self-care following the completion of your project.

In every project wherein one is required to adopt the mannerisms of an extravert, one is likely to encounter heightened levels of stress compared to their customary state. As a result, it is imperative that you allocate some time to relax and recalibrate yourself amidst different assignments. Engaging in extroverted activities on a regular basis may lead to a state of burnout, as it entails a departure from one's genuine nature. Taking periodic breaks between assignments is crucial in maintaining optimal mental well-being.

www.ingramcontent.com/pod-product-compliance
Lightning Source LLC
Chambersburg PA
CBHW050249120526
44590CB00016B/2274